Love Along The Way

Michaela Hackman

Copyright © 2016 by Michaela Hackman

All rights reserved. No part of this book may be reproduced or transmitted in any form or by any means, electronic or mechanical, including photocopying, recording, or by any information storage and retrieval system without the written permission of the author, except where permitted by law.

Any resemblance to actual persons, living or dead, or actual events in this work of poetry and prose is purely coincidental.

Printed in the U.S.A.

For Love
For Hope
...Forever

Dance with Me

Will you dance with me?

Neither of us has heard music for so long
In our hearts we hear the tune of a song
But we won't turn it up, we have too much fear
Afraid that the words won't be what we want to hear

But dancing isn't about one certain tune
All light and fluffy as we move about the room
The rhythm can change at any given turn
It doesn't mean the new dance will burn

There will be times our songs may be in contrast
Especially if we keeping singing songs of our past
Leaving the purpose of the dance to only be lost
And signals for our timing to only get crossed

Let me take your hand and move to a new melody
Your ears will hear but you must let your heart see
The beauty of our movement
As we move across the floor
Don't be afraid to let your heart crave more

Put one hand in mine and the other on my waist
Our faces together with lips close enough to taste

The sound of the music
Makes our senses come alive
Our bodies move in rhythm
Our fears are washed aside

The songs are meant to release every feeling
Some happy
Some sad
But all of them healing

We will move through this world
Dancing to our songs
Whether you lead or I
We will keep our dance strong

And when there are times your song has you blue
Just put your feet on mine and I will carry you
Until you get to a place
Where you can change the song
I'll dance with you there no matter how long

I know you would do the same for me
That's what dancing together should be

We're missing the music as we stand here and wait
We weren't meant to dance alone, that isn't our fate

I can't promise you our dance
Will always be in harmony
But if you accept that as part of life you will see

No one in this world
Will dance with you as well as me
So I'm asking you once more
Will you dance with me?

~~~~~~~~~~~

Footprints

Walk with me along this path
Of lost dreams and broken promises
Along the way we just might find
A love that will treat us kind
And a friendship that won't be left behind

We may need to reach a hand to each other
In case we stumble a bit along the way
If we don't always chose the right words to say
Let's not carrying those burdens into the next day

We can't be sure where this path will lead
But life is too short to worry too much
Let's not let our past be used as a crutch
To keep us from enjoying a touch

Leave your fears behind and walk beside me
We'll discover a life too beautiful not to share
We'll discover what it means to truly care
Let's not be afraid to take this dare

The destination can't be promised
But this I promise you
I'll treasure your heart in all that I do
And let fate and love see us through

This path will become our own
Fresh promises and new dreams
Life will be as it seems
And grace us with love redeemed

~~~~~~~~~~~

Girl Meets Boy

Why is this so hard?
Girl meets boy, boy meets girl
We start along on the right track
We swear we won't look back

We begin the path just fine
But there's fear in the back of our mind
We feel the fear of an oncoming train
Afraid our hearts will feel the strain

Others before us laid these rails
We still look upon raised nails
In the planks as if we failed
Afraid the truth will somehow tell

A story we still don't want to face
As if our life is some type of race
To the finish without being alone
But how could we have known

How hard this was going to be
To expose all our vulnerabilities
To let you be the you that you need to be
To let me be me and for us to both be free

To be who we are and not convert
We want love but our hearts stay on alert
Why can't we just erase all our past hurt
Box it up and bury in the dirt

And swear we won't look back
And start along on the right track
Boy meets girl, girl meets boy
Why is this so hard?

~~~~~~~~~~~

Baggage

I notice you on a warm spring day
You carry a bag sized like mine
Contents ...kept hidden
Packed up ...over time

We move along the same path
Making small talk about the day
We can't help but notice
We both drag our bags along the way

We don't talk about the contents
That we carry in that case
There's little we really need from there
As we stop along each place

Once in a while one of us
Opens our bag just a bit
A wound once healed reopened
The other helps to close it

The weight of our bags seem lighter
As we stroll along together
We help each other to unload
The things that won't make our lives better

We're still unsure of our destination
But the journey we will enjoy
We live one moment at a time together
A moment we won't let our bags destroy

Michaela Hackman

This morning

I woke up this morning
Wanting to feel your hand resting
On the curve of my waist
Your lips softly kissing my shoulder
Our legs laced

I kept my eyes closed
And felt your presence
Softly against my skin
Calm washed over my body
Walls of uncertainty caved in

There is no ending to this poem
It's only the beginning
When our hearts are ready to reveal
What our souls may already feel
Life will have new meaning

~~~~~~~~~~~

Serenity

Sitting in silent lucidity

Eluding what once had been

Reminders of the past forgotten

Eternity of hope awaits within

New light dawns with each fresh day

In a dreamlike state a view appears

Time stands still in sweet contemplation

Yearning for peace throughout the years

~~~~~~~~~~~~~~

Weather Rock

My weather rock tells me
All I need to know
Right now it's good…
No rain, no sleet, no snow

I can't be sure about tomorrow
I can't change it if I tried
So today I'll just enjoy
All this bright sunshine

~~~~~~~~~~~~~~

What is Love

What is Love?
When my life is falling apart around me
Knowing what it is like to have someone
Who will help me to let the pieces
Fall into their rightful place
Without letting me fall to pieces, too
That is Love

~~~~~~~~~~~

Lost In Your Eyes

Lost in your eyes I see forever
Embraced in your arms I am at peace

When I listen to your heart beat
It feels in perfect rhythm
The beat of the past has been released

To give you love
And feel you love back
A circle complete
Continuously flowing

Tomorrow is certain of only one thing
I will love you
The rest only God is knowing

I'll trust Him to lead the way
And guide us to even brighter days

Our circle of love flowing free
Right here is where I want to be

~~~~~~~~~~~~

Unexpected Gift

I wondered if I'd ever know
How to smile and laugh and love
Then an unexpected gift arrived
A gift from God above

He knew my pain, my empty soul
He wanted me to heal
He knew just what I needed
And how I needed to feel

He brought you to me on a warm spring day
But He intervened by fall
He knew if I would just take the time
My heart would begin to thaw

The greatest gift I received this year
Was given by God above
It is the greatest give I could ever want
To give and receive love

The road that led here no longer matters
What only matters is now
Many years spent preparing
But we finally learned to smile

I'll cherish this gift God gave
Your heart, your spirit, your soul
And I entrust you will do the same
Now our lives are forever whole

~~~~~~~~~~~~

Michaela Hackman

A Beautiful Place

You take me to a beautiful place
More than the eye could ever see
Inside my heart
Inside my soul
I feel beauty that will always be

Filling our lives with life and love
Warming our spirits and minds
Treating each other with tenderness
Love forever kind

A beautiful place in my sight
My smell, my taste, my touch

Inside my soul
My being
My senses feel so much

The essence of us enveloped in love
One more thing left to do
To hear the sound

"I love you"
From my lips to you

~~~~~~~~~~~~

Serendipity

Searching for ourselves we discovered each other

Eternity seemed hopeless until our path was found

Reality of obstacles in our way no longer mattered

Every new day brings music with a new sound

Never did we think we could find such happiness

Day in and day out uncertainty had loomed

In a string of events that we allowed to happen

Prepared us for the day our love began to bloom

It is the beginning of the greatest love story ever

Today and tomorrow will be better than the past

You and I stay in the moment love began at last

~~~~~~~~~~~

Michaela Hackman

Holding Hands

My hand will be holding yours
No matter where you are
If I can't be by your side
My heart is never far

From beating in rhythm with yours
Stronger every day
The bond between us grows
By your side I want to stay

So when you face those times
When life is upside down
Feel my hand in yours
And know my heart beats with the sound

Of faith, of hope, of comfort
Of compassion, truth, and love
And know your life is truly blessed
By the goodness of God above

~~~~~~~~~~~

Everything

You are everything I could ever ask for
You are all that I need
I've never felt such love before
I have no idea where this will lead

But I'll take your hand and go with you
I want to be by your side
I hope you feel the same as I do
Ready to love with arms open wide

Michaela Hackman

The Path

The path that led me to you
Was planned by God above
He took your tired heart
He filled it with my love

It began on a day in January
Cold of winter filled the air
Two barely beating hearts
Believing life unfair

Did your heart hear the sound
Of the cry of my lonesome soul?
Did my heart hear yours
Beg to once again be full?

The sound of our tears
Crying from within
Were heard by God that day
Then He chose to begin

A path meant to be traveled
We readied ourselves along the way
The stage was set for fate
But this was not a play

Our faith in one day finding
Something better than we knew
Brought us to each other
And into love a friendship grew

Each day that we're together
Is better than we thought it could ever be
Our hands now joined united
Our unchained souls forever free

Flowing

Love flows as freely as water flows over a waterfall
It's a journey to a destination
Nothing stops it

It rushes past obstacles
It finds paths where none before had existed
It brings beauty with every touch and every sound

It's the journey that creates the beauty
Anticipation to the destination creates excitement

Obstacles create dimension
Paths create breadth

The waterfall needs both the land and water
To create it's magic

Love needs two different, willing souls
To create it's magic

Making the journey together
Anticipating the best

Working out obstacles
Unafraid of the path ahead

~~~~~~~~~~~~

Every Day

My every day begins and ends
With beautiful thoughts of you
The warm embrace of your love
Each day carries me through

Whatever storm approaches
You shelter me from it all
Your calm voice
Your gentle touch
Your love won't let me fall

You lift me up higher
Than I imagined I'd ever be
I hope that you in turn will know
That same feeling of love from me

Michaela Hackman

Nowhere Else

There is nowhere else I'd rather be
Than having you sit here next to me
Listening to the waves crash against the sand
I hope time will pass with us hand in hand

But for now I want time to stand still
With endless joy our hearts will fill
And carry us through all of life's ups and downs
Giving us peace from all that we are bound

There's nowhere else I'd rather be
Than sitting with you next to me
But when this adventure comes to an end
A new journey of joy is sure to begin

~~~~~~~~~~~

On Top Of the World

I feel like I'm on top of the world
Uplifted
Floating
While reaching high above
Endless potential
But rooted in your love

The embrace of your arms
While I fly free
The feeling of acceptance
I can be me

I now can see forever
Nothing is in my way
My new vision gives me hope to see
The brightness of each day

You will be my anchor
But allow me needed wings
To be all I'm meant to be
So that my soul forever sings

~~~~~~~~~~~~

Who He Is

I know who I am searching for
When he looks me in the eyes
I know how that look will make me feel
His eyes will not disguise

The amazing vision before him
His longing to reach out
To take me into his warm embrace
Erasing all of my doubt

That loves fails to exist in this world
Filled with envy, pride, and greed
He's a man still true in virtues
Willing to give me what I need

Honesty, faithfulness, integrity
Patience, kindness indeed
Virtues of a real man
Worthy to walk by my side at my speed

He'll be a man deserving
Of all that I have to give
Together we'll create a life
Better than we thought we could ever live

~~~~~~~~~~~~

Angel

A
New
Gift with
Each new
Light of day

Angel
I believe it
Because when you look at me
All I can see is love in your eyes
Deep love

As if you are seeing it
Feeling it
For the first time
Savoring it
Knowing it
Embracing it
A gift you are grateful for
A gift you treasure
A gift you will cherish always
And with each new day
Your eyes will see it again
Your angel, me

~~~~~~~~~~~

If

If each day I wrote you a love letter
To tell you what you mean to me
Would your eyes tire of it
Or look forward to the words you will see?

If each night I kissed you goodnight
With lips that long for you
Would your lips tire of it
Or desire to feel it too?

If each morning you awoke
To the feel of my loving touch
Would your body tire of it
Or would you not mind so much?

You give to me selflessly
I want to give back to you
The comfort of my love
Each day as if it's new

~~~~~~~~~~~

Soulmate

Songs of tomorrow sound so sweet

Our new life just beginning

Undeniable connection between our souls

Love made our hearts start singing

Many years passed awaiting this time

Another life seems so far away

Time stands still while we're in each other's arms

Eternity is sweetened each day

~~~~~~~~~~~

Broken Pieces

Broken pieces of yesterday
Won't get in the way
With each sweet kiss we share
The pieces go away

Replaced with light
And love
And grace
Every time you touch my face

My heart feels warmth it never knew
My soul is no longer lost and blue

Your love has shown me how to live
How to love
How to give

I feel fulfilled
Full of love and grace
Your love takes me to a new place

That's where we'll stay
For all the days
Two hearts as one
Our life has just begun

Fill My Heart

You fill my heart with your every glance
Your breath fills the depth of my soul
A gift from God you are to me
Released from the past and its toll

A new start
A new life
Living each day with new eyes
Feeling love and loving you
Together creating new lives

I don't know what tomorrow brings
But my faith now holds steadfast
I believe you are a part of my life
That is meant to forever last

~~~~~~~~~~~

Uncover

You uncover me
Open my soul to possibility
Never before have I seen
This beautiful world before me

You wrap me in your arms
A smile revealing your charm
A warm heart causing no harm
Allowing my thoughts to disarm

You love me
With you I feel free
Free to be who I am meant to be
Happily no end in sight do I see

~~~~~~~~~~~

A New Year

A wondrous year ahead
Beauty in each day
A life filled with joy
An amazing journey along the way

To know and feel such love
Is a gift we're blessed to receive
How grateful to live each day
With hope and faith, in God we believe

Our love is sure to grow
And go on for many years
Each day we awake with joy
And in our hearts keep each other near

One Day

One day it will be over
I won't get to see your face
... to hear your laugh
....to touch your skin
To never again embrace

I dread that day
I don't want it near
...to say goodbye
...to be apart
Loneliness I so deeply fear

Til then I want to love you fiercely
Day in and day out
...to feel your love
...to give you love
Living out what life is truly about

Take my hand and walk with me
Through this life of true unknowns
...love
...not fear
Will get us through
All that life will try to throw

We'll make it through
To the other side
...God's Grace
...Eternal Peace
But know, my love,
Even at that time
My love will never cease

Michaela Hackman

Take Flight

When you touch my face
And look into my eyes
I see something I never before saw

Your eyes tell me that without a doubt
You will catch me if I fall

So I will just take flight
And fly across the sky
Knowing in your arms I'll safely land

Your love
Your warmth
Your kindness
Give my wings room to expand

We'll deal with life's ups and downs
When it's time to reach the ground
By your side I'll be grateful
To share in the love we have found

~~~~~~~~~~~~

My Last Love

I want you to be my last love
The last one I ever kiss
I want to be the one you crave
And fill your days with endless bliss

I want to start each morning
With the vision of your face
And feeling of your strong arms
Holding my body in a warm embrace

All the days we have left to live
I want to be by your side
To love and laugh
And live and give
God's grace will be our guide

And when the day comes
To take our last breath
To go to our heavenly home
I hope it's silently in our sleep
Exhausted from our worldly roam

~~~~~~~~~~~~

The Beginning

I looked at you as you looked into my eyes
You softly spoke
Your words were a surprise

Passion and beautiful
Are words you would say
To describe your time with me
In an appreciative way

The warmth of your face melted my heart
I wondered at that moment
If it was just the start

The beginning of the greatest love story ever
Or the worst heartbreak
Falling for words so cleaver

The fear could not stop my thought
From wanting to see all that I sought

You showed me your soul
Humble and true
I knew at that moment
Where I needed to be was with you

Months have passed
Time has flown
With a passion for living
Oh how our love has grown!

The beginning of the greatest love story ever
Led us from storms we could no longer weather

We hopped on the rainbow
And found our pot of gold
A friend
A lover
A partner
With whom to grow old

~~~~~~~~~~~

Michaela Hackman

Endless Love

A new beginning
A love endless flows
A season of change
New life together grows

Warmth of the sun
Brings color to each day
If hidden behind the clouds
Love doesn't go away

Falling for you
Destination unknown
I can see it all from high above
A new dawn
A new light
A new journey
Forever
Sharing endless love

~~~~~~~~~~~

Knowing

If I had known how this love would go
I would have shared it in a song
If I could have seen where this path would lead
I would have followed it all along

But knowing me
And all the fears I felt
I would not have believed possible
The true bliss your love gives to me
You make my world complete and full

I'll take your hand and you'll take mine
Together we'll face all that's yet to come
The road ahead is sure to wind
Our love has merged two souls as one

~~~~~~~~~~~

Late At Night

I know it's late
But I can't go to sleep right now
I can't get you off of my mind

Every time I try
I keep circling back to you
Your eyes
Your touch
The way you make me feel
Completely loved

I don't want to go to sleep
I don't want to stop thinking about you
And how you make me feel
I want this to be real
But if I close my eyes

I'm afraid I'll awake to find
You were only just a dream

How sweet it seems
That I can be loved by someone
As amazing as you
And it not be just a dream

If you are just a dream
I want to go on awake
With my eyes wide open
And my heart in your hands

Because every moment thinking of you
Is way too sweet
Than to ever think ordinary dreams
Ever could compete

Michaela Hackman

Tell Me

When you tell me that you love me
A whisper from your lips
With words I long to hear
It lifts me
It comforts me
I crave you to be near

When you take me in your arms
And hold me tender and tight
Loving me
Inspiring me
My heart sings as it takes flight

It's what your love does to me
I can't imagine life any other way
I'm blessed and love you back the same
Every single day

I Believe In Love

I'm in a place I've heard of

But never been before
Enveloped in a warm embrace
Longing to feel more
In an endless swirl of passion
Ever changing growing strong
Varied paths we traveled
Ending up right where we belong

Incredible sense of comfort
Now I know just how it feels

Love beyond my imagination
Oh how lucky! This is real!
Valentines, all the days yet to come
Endless love, two hearts in rhythm beat as one

~~~~~~~~~~~

Years Ago

Years ago
I never thought I would be here today
Feeling the incredible love you so freely give to me

Years ago
I couldn't have imagined my head
Fitting so comfortably on your chest
And your strong arms holding me close

Years ago
I didn't think it possible
I didn't think such love existed
I told myself I didn't need it

Today
I can't imagine living without you

Years from now
I'll look back at the time before I knew you
And realize it was all about sowing the seeds
For the best that was yet to come

Years from now
I will see how the beauty of our love
Blossomed throughout our intertwined lives

Becoming the wondrous garden in which we live

Today

I am grateful as I stand by your side
As we love
As we live
In this garden we call ours

~~~~~~~~~~~~

Michaela Hackman

My Umbrella

I haven't felt the rain since we met
I've seen it fall all around me
The lightning strikes nearby
The thunder vibrates the ground
But not a drop do I feel

It's not that you shield me
From the storms that come with life
Allowing me to live obliviously

Rather you stand beside me
Believing in me
Loving me

Creating an umbrella
So I can continue to dance
While the rain waters life around me
Helping me to make sense of the storm

~~~~~~~~~~~~

Each Morning

Each morning when I wake
My first thought is of you
Rare a dawn arrives when it's not
Hoping on your mind I am too

Wishing to hear but also feel
Your breath whisper my name
Wanting to see the look in your eyes
As you look at me the same

Filling me with love complete
Your touch
Your voice
Your eyes
A feeling I have never known
And couldn't explain if I tried

This longing that I feel for you
Is deep right to my core
I never want to feel it end
I want you more and more

When that day comes
And I awake to my wish come true
Endless joy will fill my heart
As I awake next to you

~~~~~~~~~~~~

The Sunrise

When I saw the sunrise this morning
The gold burst ready to reveal itself to the world
Bringing light
Bringing warmth
Bringing beauty to a new day
Creating a sky of colors swirled

I thought of you as I watched the transition
The haze in the sky formed like blue waves
Covering the ball
Rising steadily
Working its way higher
Moving toward what it craves

White fog like a cloud
That had dropped out of the sky
Lingering above the green field

A beautiful picture
Painted
For only a moment
As that sun in the sky refused to yield

A magnificent vision
Captured forever

Stays in my mind and in my heart
Just as time with you
No matter how much or how few
Remains a beautiful picture
Even when we are apart

Joyful

I found in you joyfulness
Elation beyond belief
My whole life I have waited
To feel some relief

From living inside myself
Begging to break out
To experience all I've heard
True love to be about

Finding you was a journey
That started first within my soul
A path that had to start
With me making myself whole

A hard look
A firm hand
My heavy heart began to rise
Before I knew it
My look inside
Set my outside up to thrive

The time came
You appeared to me
Your heart held in your hand

You offered to me all of your love
While by my side you pledged to stand

Not a regret
Not a day goes by
Without being thankful for this grace
Rapture barely begins to describe
The delight of being in this place

To feel such bliss
Seems like a dream
One I hope will never end
In you I found more than I have ever wished
A lover and a friend

~~~~~~~~~~~

I Love

I love
Sunshine when it rains
Clouds breaking away
Dancing in your arms

I love
Mist on a mountain top
Leaves floating mid air
You singing your charms

I love
Crispness of the fall
Our heat like the summer
Newness of the springtime

I love
Everything about you
Every moment by your side
Describing our love in rhyme

~~~~~~~~~~~~

Second Chances

Second chances
At life
At love
Second chances
Grace from above

No longer held back
By strife, by fear
Looking forward
To many good years

New hope
New dreams
Along the way
Finding contentment
In each new day

This life I've been given
I will make it through
I will live
I will love
Grateful for God's grace
And for you

~~~~~~~~~~~~

Michaela Hackman

Simply Love

What if we viewed love like we do the sun?
Each morning we're graced
With the beauty of its entrance into our world
As it offers a painted sky that is different
From the days past

Curious as to how it will affect our day
Sad when it doesn't show up
But comforted to know it's only behind a cloud

In awe of its mid-day brilliance
And ability to provide warmth and help things grow
Inspired by its majestic setting
And the peacefulness it brings
Knowing it will return tomorrow

Could love be that simple?

Yes

You asked and I said yes
Yes to tomorrow
While today is still fresh

Yes to possibility
To hopes and to dreams
Yes to our love
And to everything that means

Yes to accepting the wounds of our past
Yes to doing everything to make our love last

Yes to the good
The bad
The mundane
Yes to the days we'll drive each other insane

Yes
Because everything about our love makes life new

Yes
Because I can't see tomorrow without you

~~~~~~~~~~

The Beginning

....because there is never an end to love

ABOUT THE AUTHOR

Michaela Hackman is a native of Latrobe, Pennsylvania and currently resides in the upstate of South Carolina. Her dream when she was 10 years old was to travel the world to take pictures and write stories. Long ago she put down the pen, picking it up 25 years later with the compassion and grace of a woman who has seen the world, both the good and the bad. Her poetry symbolizes the search for being true to one's self. Her writing is intended to help ordinary people to find hope, and to not feel so alone as they struggle to deal with obstacles in their lives.

www.ingramcontent.com/pod-product-compliance
Lightning Source LLC
Chambersburg PA
CBHW061248040426
42444CB00010B/2297